M000281918

TOfU! TOfU! TOfU!

CHINESE STYLE

AUTHOR
Mu-Tsun Lee

EDITOR
Huang Su-Huei

EDITORIAL STAFF
Sophia Lin
Yen-Jen Lai
John Holt

TRANSLATION
Innie Hua

ART DIRECTION
F.S. Chang

PHOTOGRAPHY
Aki Ohno

DESIGN
AGP Productions Inc.

WEI-CHUAN PUBLISHING
1455 Monterey Pass Rd., #110
Monterey Park, CA 91754, U.S.A.
Tel: (213)261-3880 (213)261-3878
Fax: (213)261-3299

2nd Fl., 28 Section 4, Jen-Ai Road
Taipei, Taiwan, R.O.C.
Tel: (02)702-1148 (02)702-1149
Fax: (02)704-2729

PRINTED IN TAIWAN, R.O.C.

COPYRIGHT © 1994
By Wei-Chuan Publishing
All rights reserved.
No portion of this book may be reproduced
by any means without the permission of the
publisher.

Notice: Information contained in this book is
accurate and complete to the best of our
knowledge. All recommendations are made
with no guarantees on the part of the
authors or Wei-Chuan Publishing. The
authors and publisher disclaim all liability in
connection with the use or misuse of this
information.

FIRST PRINTING, OCTOBER 1994
ISBN 0-941676-49-8

作者
李木村

總編輯
黃淑惠

文稿協助
林淑華、賴燕眞、何久恩

翻譯
華茵

設計策劃
張方馨

攝影
大野現

設計
AGP Productions Inc.

電腦排版
甘露資訊印刷有限公司

印刷
中華彩色印刷股份有限公司

味全出版社有限公司
台北市仁愛路4段28號2樓
郵政劃撥00182038號味全出版社帳
電話： (02) 702-1148. (02) 702-1149
傳眞： (02) 704-2729

版權所有
局版台業字第0179號
中華民國83年10月初版
定價：新台幣壹佰貳拾元整

Contents 目 錄

Conversion Tables 量 器 介 紹

1 C. (1 cup) = 236 c.c.   1 杯 = 236 c.c.

1 T. (1 tablespoon) = 15 c.c.   1 大匙 = 15 c.c.

1 t. (1 teaspoon) = 5 c.c.   1 小匙 = 5 c.c.

Recipe measurements in this book (pp.8 thru 77) are designed for two servings.

本食譜份量爲二人份

Soybean Products 黃豆製品介紹

1 **SOFT TOFU** is tender and suitable as an appetizer and excellent when steamed, deep-fried or served as soup.
2 **HARD TOFU** is firmer and more suitable for deep-frying or cooking in sauces. However hard or soft tofu may be used according to one's preference if not specified in the recipe.
■ Pat tofu dry before frying or deep-frying.
■ Prepare tofu salad just prior to serving the meal to avoid watery tofu.
■ Retaining unused tofu in water, in a clean container, will keep it fresh for several days Be sure to change the water daily.

1 **嫩豆腐：**品質較嫩，適於冷食、蒸、炸或煮湯。
2 **硬豆腐：**品質稍硬，適於炒、炸或紅燒。書內若不指定使用嫩或硬豆腐，可依喜好選用。
■ 用來煎或炸的豆腐，應事先拭乾水份才使用。
■ 涼拌豆腐應食前才做，以免豆腐出水。
■ 豆腐沒用完時，放入有水的容器內，每天換水，可保持新鮮數天。

3   **BEAN CURD SKIN (FU PEA)** is made by mashing soybeans with water, then cooking. The membrane formed on top is the fresh bean curd pouch (For recipe, see p.43). Dried bean curd skin is achieved when the fresh pouch is allowed to dry. (For recipes, see pp. 23, 71).

4   **PRESSED BEAN CURD:** white pressed bean curd is made by dehydrating tofu. To make savory pressed bean curd, cook white pressed bean curd with a spice pouch. (For recipes, see pp. 17, 29, 31, 33) All recipes in this book require the use of savory pressed bean curd. If white bean curd is used instead, add a little salt.

5, 6   **BEAN CURD STRIPS** and **BEAN CURD SHEETS** ("Bai Yeh") differ only in shape. Uses for both are the same. (For recipes, see pp 21, 33, 35, 77).

3   **腐皮：**黃豆加水磨成漿，煮過後浮在表面凝成一層薄膜即爲新鮮腐皮，又稱豆包（食譜見43頁）；乾燥後即成乾腐皮（食譜見23、71頁）

4   **豆乾：**豆腐脫水後即成白豆乾，放入五香滷汁內滷過即成五香豆乾（食譜見17、29、31、33頁）。書內的菜餚均以五香豆乾試做，故若使用白豆乾，菜內宜略加鹽

5, 6   **干絲、百頁：**僅形狀不同，用途大同小異（食譜見21、33、35、77頁）。

Soy Milk
豆漿

1 Rinse 2 c. soybeans and soak in 6 c. water for 6 hours.

2 Rinse soybeans after they have expanded 2 to 2.5 times original size. Then drain.

3 Add 6 c. water to soaked soybeans. Divide them in 3 portions and liquify in a blender.

4 Add additional 6 c. water to the liquified beans then pour into a cheesecloth bag. Squeeze out liquid to make raw soy milk. Bring the milk to boil then reduce heat to medium; cook 10 minutes (stir constantly to prevent sticking to pan). Add sugar for sweet soy milk. It is an excellent substitute for dairy milk.

■ Cooked soy milk can be used to make tofu, tofu pudding, bean curd skin, or other soy bean products.

1 黃豆2杯洗淨加水6杯浸泡6小時。

2 黃豆膨脹2-2.5倍再洗淨，瀝乾水份。

3 泡好的黃豆加水6杯，分三次攪碎。

4 再加水6杯，全部倒入布袋內，將汁擠出即為生豆漿。生豆漿燒開，改中火續煮10分鐘（煮時須攪拌，以免粘鍋）加糖即成甜豆漿，是為很好的牛奶取代品。

■ 煮好的豆漿可製造豆腐、豆腐花或豆腐皮等豆類製品。

Tofu
豆腐的製造方法

12 c. soy milk (p. 6)

| 1 | 1 T. gypsum |
| | 1 c. warm water |

豆漿（見6頁）……………12杯

| 1 | 燒石膏 ……………………1大匙 |
| | 溫水 ……………………………1杯 |

1 Bring soy milk to boil, stirring simultaneously to prevent sticking; turn off heat. Add mixture  slowly to hot soy milk while stirring. Let stand 10 minutes until mixture solidifies.

2 Place white cloth on a mold.

3 Put the solidified mixture in the mold until 90% filled.

4 Fold the cloth over to cover the mixture then add the wooden cover. Place 3 lbs of weight on top for 15 minutes to press the water out. Remove wooden cover and cloth to finish tofu.

1 將豆漿燒開即熄火（煮時須攪動，以免粘鍋），趁熱徐徐加入拌勻的 1 料，邊攪拌至完全加完，立即停止攪拌，靜置10分鐘至凝固即成豆腐腦。

2 將白布鋪在模型上。

3 倒入豆腐腦至九分滿。

4 將白布覆蓋好，蓋上木板蓋，上加2公斤重壓，使水份濾出（約15分鐘），除去模型及白布即為豆腐。

½ lb. (225g) tofu

1 total of 2 T. as desired:
  salmon caviar,
  frozen seasoned capein roe,
  dried shrimp,
  pickled mustard greens,
  green onion

2 3 T. nori paste
5 T. water

豆腐 ……………………6兩（225公克）

鮭魚卵、飛魚卵、蝦米、
榨菜、青蔥 ………任選共2大匙

紫菜醬 ………………………3大匙
水 ……………………………5大匙

Tofu With Nori Paste
紫菜醬豆腐

1 Cut tofu in pieces then place on a plate. Put ❶ on top then spread on mixture ❷ .

1 豆腐切塊置盤，上置 ❶ 料，淋上調勻的 ❷ 料食用。

Tofu With Dried Shrimp
榨菜蝦米豆腐

1 Rinse and soak 2 T. each of pickled mustard greens and dried shrimp for 5 minutes. Remove and mince.

2 Heat 1/2 T. sesame oil. Stir-fry shrimp; add in mustard greens,1 t. soy sauce and 1 T. minced green onion. Mix well and sprinkle on tofu.

1 將榨菜、蝦米共2大匙分別洗淨，泡水5分鐘撈出剁碎。

2 麻油 1/2 大匙燒熱，先炒蝦米，隨入榨菜、醬油1小匙、蔥末1大匙拌勻，撒在豆腐上即成。

½ lb. (225g) soft tofu

½ apple

½ pineapple

4 T. salmon Caviar

1

¾ t. each: sugar, salt
2 T. vinegar or lemon juice
⅙ t. pepper
6 T. oil

10

嫩豆腐	6兩（225公克）
蘋果	1/2個
鳳梨	1/2個
鮭魚卵	4大匙
糖、鹽	各3/4小匙
醋或檸檬汁	2大匙
胡椒	1/6小匙
沙拉油	6大匙

Tofu & Caviar in Pineapple

鮭魚卵鳳梨豆腐

1   Dice tofu, slice apple. Hollow out pineapple, dice the pulp, and save the pineapple skin for later use.

2   Put tofu, apple and pineapple into hollowed out pineapple with salmon caviar on top. Spread on mixture ❶ and serve.

1   將豆腐切丁，蘋果切片，鳳梨挖取出果肉後切丁，鳳梨皮留用。

2   將豆腐、蘋果及鳳梨裝入鳳梨皮內，上置鮭卵，淋上調勻的 ❶ 料食用。

½ lb. (225g) shredded hard tofu or pressed bean curd

1 total of 2 c. as desired: bean sprouts, shredded ham, celery, cucumber, carrot, bamboo shoots, mushrooms and nappa cabbage.

2
3 T. sesame paste or peanut butter
1 T. sesame oil or cooking oil
3 T. soy sauce
2 T. vinegar or lemon juice
½ T. sugar
1 t. each (minced): green onion, garlic clove

4 T. mixed nuts

硬豆腐或豆乾(切絲) ‧‧‧‧‧‧‧‧6兩
(225公克)

綠豆芽、火腿、芹菜、黃瓜、
紅蘿蔔、筍、洋菇、
大白菜 ‧‧‧‧‧‧‧‧‧‧任選切絲共2杯

芝麻醬或花生醬 ‧‧‧‧‧‧‧‧‧‧3大匙
麻油或沙拉油 ‧‧‧‧‧‧‧‧‧‧‧‧1大匙
醬油 ‧‧‧‧‧‧‧‧‧‧‧‧‧‧‧‧‧‧‧‧‧‧‧‧3大匙
醋或檸檬汁 ‧‧‧‧‧‧‧‧‧‧‧‧‧‧‧2大匙
糖 ‧‧‧‧‧‧‧‧‧‧‧‧‧‧‧‧‧‧‧‧‧‧‧‧‧‧‧‧‧$1/_2$大匙
蔥、蒜末 ‧‧‧‧‧‧‧‧‧‧‧‧‧‧‧‧各1小匙

綜合硬果仁 ‧‧‧‧‧‧‧‧‧‧‧‧‧‧‧‧4大匙

Tofu Salad

豆腐沙拉

1   Place shredded tofu on plate; surround with **1** . When serving, sprinkle with mixture **2** and mixed nuts.

■   Ready-made salad dressings or salad dressings and sauces (pp. 8,9) from Wei-Chuan's "Chinese Cooking Made Easy" may be used for mixture **2** .

1   豆腐絲置盤中,將 **1** 料排列周圍,食用時酌量淋上調勻的 **2** 料,並撒上綜合硬果仁食用。

■   可買現成的沙拉醬或選用「速簡中國菜」各種沙拉醬、汁(見8、9頁)來取代 **2** 料。

½ lb. (225g) soft tofu

1 avocado

① ½ T. mustard powder
1 ½ T. soy sauce
1 T. water

① ½ c. hard tofu
½ c. canned tuna
6 mushrooms, sliced
Total 6 T. minced onion, green
  red peppers
4 T. salad dressing

2 T. cooked sesame seeds or
  ground peanuts

6 slices of lettuce

14

嫩豆腐 ·············6兩(225公克)

奶果 ····················1個

①
芥末粉 ·····················¹/₂大匙
醬油 ····················1 ¹/₂大匙
水 ·······················1大匙

硬豆腐 ·····················¹/₂杯
罐頭鮪魚 ···················¹/₂杯
① 洋菇(切片) ·················6個
青紅椒、洋蔥 ······切碎共6大匙
沙拉醬 ·····················4大匙

熟芝麻或花生（壓碎）······2大匙

生菜 ·······················6片

Tofu & Avocado With Mustard
芥末奶果豆腐

1 Remove skin and seed from avocado. Cut tofu and avocado into pieces then place on a plate. Spread on mixture **①** and serve.

1 奶果去皮、籽後與豆腐分別切小塊置盤，淋上調勻的 **①** 料食用。

Tofu & Tuna With Lettuce
豆腐鮪魚生菜包

1 Mash the tofu and squeeze out water. Drain tuna.

2 Gently mix **①** well and sprinkle with sesame seeds then serve with lettuce.

1 硬豆腐壓碎並擠乾水份；鮪魚瀝乾水份備用。

2 將 **①** 料輕輕拌勻，撒上芝麻後，用生菜包食。

½ lb. (225g) pressed bean curd

1 | ½ T. soy sauce
1 T. sesame oil

2 | 2 T. shredded green onion
1 T. minced coriander
1 shredded red chili

豆乾 ················6兩 (225公克)	

❶	醬油 ·······················¹/₂大匙	
	麻油 ························1大匙	

❷	蔥絲 ·······················2大匙	
	香菜(切碎) ·················1大匙	
	紅辣椒絲 ····················1條	

Pressed Bean Curd Salad

涼拌豆乾

1 Shred the pressed bean curd. Mix with ❶ and ❷. Serve.

■ 1/2 t. chili paste may be used for shredded red chili of ❷.

1 豆乾切絲,拌入 ❶ 料及 ❷ 料即成。

■ 可用辣椒醬¹/₂小匙來取代紅辣椒絲。

½ lb. (225g) soft tofu

2 preserved eggs

1 T. minced coriander or green onion

1 1 T. soy sauce
1 t. sesame oil

嫩豆腐 ·············6兩 (225公克)

皮蛋 ·······················2個

香菜或蔥 (切碎) ···········1大匙

醬油露或醬油 ·············1大匙
麻油 ·······················1小匙

Tofu & Preserved Eggs

皮蛋豆腐

1 Dice tofu and preserved eggs then place on a plate. Put coriander on top then spread with mixture **❶**.

1 將豆腐、皮蛋分別切丁置盤，上置香菜，淋上調均的 **❶** 料食用。

Tofu & Salted Eggs

鹹蛋豆腐

1 Substitute preserved eggs with salted eggs (cooked), and reduce soy sauce to 1 t.. Other ingredients and procedures are the same as "Tofu & Preserved Eggs", above.

1 將皮蛋改用鹹蛋 (煮熟)，醬油改1小匙，其他材料做法如上。

⅓ lb. (150g) bean curd strips

1. 2 t. baking soda
   4 c. water

2. total of 1 c. as desired: bean sprouts, sliced mushrooms, shredded carrot, celery, red & green bell peppers.

3. ½ t. each: salt, sugar
   1 T. sesame oil

干絲 ················4兩（150公克）

1 小蘇打 ················2小匙
   水 ··················4杯

2 綠豆芽、洋菇（切片）、紅蘿蔔、
   芹菜或西芹、青紅椒
   ·················切絲任選共1杯

3 鹽、糖 ··············各½小匙
   麻油 ················1大匙

Bean Curd Strips Salad

涼拌干絲

1 Bring ❶ to boil and turn off heat immediately. Add bean curd strips; stir until soft and color turns white (Soaking time may vary from 1 to 20 minutes depending on the brand of the strips).

2 Blanch ❷ in boiling water for 30 seconds then rinse briefly under cold water. Drain; mix well with bean curd strips and ❸. Serve.

1 將 ❶ 料燒開即熄火，放入干絲，時時翻拌至呈白色且軟硬適度（視廠牌的不同，泡的時間約由1分鐘到20分鐘不等），撈出沖洗至無蘇打味。

2 將 ❷ 料放入滾水內略燙（約30秒），再用冷水沖涼，瀝乾水份與干絲及 ❸ 料拌勻即可。

4 sheets of dried bean curd skin,
6"X 8" (15 cm X 20 cm)

1 | total of ½ lb. (225g): bean
sprouts, shredded carrots

2 | ¼ t. salt
1 t. sesame oil

3 | 1 T. each: flour, water

4 | 1 ½ T. soy sauce
1 t. each: sugar, vinegar
½ t. chili oil

Vegetarian Bean Curd Rolls

煎腐皮捲

乾腐皮 (15公分 × 20公分) …4張

1 | 綠豆芽、紅蘿蔔絲 ………共6兩
　　　　　　　　　　　　　(225公克)

2 | 鹽 …………………………¼小匙
　 | 麻油 ………………………1小匙

3 | 麵粉、水 ………………各1大匙

4 | 醬油膏或醬油 …………1½大匙
　 | 糖、醋 …………………各1小匙
　 | 辣油 ……………………………½小匙

1 Blanch ① in boiling water briefly; remove and mix with ②. Divide the mixture into 4 portions (filling). Mix ③.

2 Place a portion of filling in each bean curd skin; then fold the skin and wrap the filling to form a baton. Seal the edge of the skin with mixture ③.

3 Heat 3 T. oil; fry bean curd rolls in low heat (to prevent burning) 2 minutes until both sides turn golden brown. Remove and cut in sections. Spread mixture ④ over bean curd rolls. Serve.

■ If bean curd skin is too dry, cover with a wet cloth until soft.

1 將 ① 料用滾水川燙後撈出，拌入 ② 料分成四等份做餡；③ 料調勻成麵糊。

2 每張乾腐皮放入一份餡，捲成長條狀，以麵糊黏住封口，依次捲好。

3 油3大匙燒熱，將腐皮捲以小火 (以免燒焦) 煎約2分鐘至兩面呈金黃色取出切段，淋上拌勻 ④ 料即成。

■ 腐皮如太乾，可覆蓋濕巾待柔軟後再使用。

½ lb. (225g) hard tofu

1
⅛ t. pepper
1 T. flour

2
½ T. sugar
2 T. soy sauce
1 T. cooking wine

3
total of 1 c., (cut in pieces):
mushrooms, onion, green &
red bell peppers

硬豆腐 ··············6兩 (225公克)

胡椒 ·······················1/8小匙
麵粉 ·························1大匙

糖 ··························1/2大匙
醬油 ·······················2大匙
酒 ···························1大匙

洋菇、洋蔥、靑紅椒 切塊共1杯

Tofu Steak
煎豆腐排

1 Pat tofu dry and sprinkle with **1**.

2 Heat 1 T. oil. Fry tofu over medium heat 5 minutes until both sides are golden brown. Add **2** then turn over; continue to fry for 1 minute. Remove and put on a serving plate.

3 Heat 1 T. oil, briefly stir-fry **3** with 1 T. water, pinch of salt and pepper. Remove and place around the tofu.

1 豆腐拭乾水份，撒上 **1** 料。

2 油1大匙燒熱，將豆腐用中火煎約5分鐘至兩面呈金黃色，放入 **2** 料翻面續煎1分鐘置盤。

3 油1大匙燒熱，將 **3** 料加水1大匙，鹽、胡椒少許略炒拌，置於豆腐旁即可。

Fried Tofu
煎豆腐

1 Slice tofu in 1/2" (1.5 cm) thickness. Sprinkle with 1/4 t. each of pepper and salt. Fry tofu 5 minutes until both sides turn golden brown.

1 豆腐切1.5公分薄片，撒上胡椒、鹽各1/4小匙，煎至兩面呈金黃色即成。

½ lb. (225g) tofu

¼ c. flour

1 egg, beaten

1 T. minced green onion

1 t. minced ginger root

1 ½ t. salt
1 t. each: cooking wine,
    sesame oil
½ c. stock

26

豆腐 ⋯⋯⋯⋯⋯⋯6兩 (225公克)

麵粉 ⋯⋯⋯⋯⋯⋯⋯⋯⋯¹/₄杯

鷄蛋 (打勻) ⋯⋯⋯⋯⋯⋯1個

蔥 (切碎) ⋯⋯⋯⋯⋯⋯1大匙

薑 (切碎) ⋯⋯⋯⋯⋯⋯1小匙

鹽 ⋯⋯⋯⋯⋯⋯⋯⋯⋯¹/₃小匙
酒、麻油 ⋯⋯⋯⋯⋯各1小匙
高湯或水 ⋯⋯⋯⋯⋯⋯¹/₂杯

Peking-style Fried Tofu

鍋塌豆腐

1   Pat tofu dry then cut in slices, 1/2" (1.5 cm) thick. Before frying, coat the slices with flour then egg.

2   Heat 2 T. oil. Arrange coated slices evenly on wok. Fry over medium heat 1 minute. Turn over and fry until both sides are golden brown. Add in green onion, ginger root and ❶. Pierce tofu with a fork to allow liquid to seep through. Cook until liquid is evaporated. Sprinkle on hot bean paste or soy sauce if desired, then serve.

1   豆腐拭乾水份，切1.5公分厚片，煎時先沾上麵粉，再沾上打勻的蛋液。

2   油2大匙燒熱，將豆腐一片片整齊排在鍋底，用中火煎約1分鐘翻面，再煎至兩面呈金黃色，放入蔥、薑及 ❶ 料，用叉子叉透豆腐 (使其入味)，煮至汁收乾，可淋辣豆瓣醬或醬油食用。

⅓ lb. (150g) beef

1 1 t. each: soy sauce, cooking wine
1 t. cornstarch

2 2 T. shredded green onion
¼ c. pre-softened Chinese black mushrooms, shredded
¼ lb. (115g) pressed bean curd, shredded

3 total of ¾ c. (shredded): green & red bell pepper, bamboo shoots (or your choice of vegetables)

4 ½ t. sugar
pinch of pepper
½ T. each: cooking wine, sesame oil
1 T. soy sauce
1 t. chili paste

牛肉 ……………4兩(150公克)

醬油、酒 ……………各1小匙
太白粉 ………………1小匙

蔥絲 ………………2大匙
泡軟的香菇絲 ………………¼杯
豆乾(切絲) ………3兩(115公克)

青紅椒絲、筍絲
(或任選蔬菜) ……………共¾杯

糖 ………………½小匙
胡椒 ………………少許
酒、麻油 ………………各½大匙
醬油 ………………1大匙
辣椒醬 ………………1小匙

Pressed Bean Curd & Beef

香干炒肉絲

1 Shred beef then mix with ❶ .

2 Heat 2 T. oil. Stir-fry ❷ until fragrant. Add beef and stir-fry until separated and cooked. Add ❸ and stir-fry 30 seconds. Add mixture ❹ ; stir to mix well.

1 牛肉切絲，調入 ❶ 料。

2 油2大匙燒熱，炒香 ❷ 料，隨入肉絲炒開至熟，續入 ❸ 料炒約30秒再加調勻的 ❹ 料炒拌均勻即成。

Pressed Bean Curd & Chicken

豆乾炒鷄丁

1 Use chicken for beef. Add 1 t. cornstarch and 3 T. water in ❹ . Other ingredients and procedures are the same as the above recipe.

1 將牛肉改用鷄肉，切丁； ❹ 料多加太白粉1小匙、水3大匙，其他材料做法同上。

1
¼ lb. (115g) pressed bean curd, sliced
¼ lb. (115g) lean chicken, beef or pork (sliced)

⅓ lb. (150g) cabbage, cut in pieces

8 slices of fresh garlic or garlic clove (sliced diagonally)

2
½ t. sugar
½ T. each: cooking wine, sesame oil
¾ T. each: soy sauce, sweet bean paste
1 t. chili paste

豆乾 (切片) ………3兩 (115公克)
瘦肉 (鷄、牛或豬)切片 ……3兩
　　　　　　　　　　　(115公克)

包心菜 (切塊) ……4兩 (150公克)

蒜苗或蒜 (切斜片) …………8片

糖 ……………………………1/2小匙
酒、麻油 ………………各1/2大匙
醬油、甜麵醬 …………各3/4大匙
辣椒醬 ………………………1小匙

Pressed Bean Curd & Cabbage

豆乾炒包心菜

1 Heat 1 T. oil. Stir-fry cabbage with 1/8 t. salt until soft; add 1 T. water if too dry; remove. Wipe wok dry.

2 Heat 2 T. oil. Stir-fry garlic until fragrant; add ① and stir-fry until meat is cooked and bean curd turns golden brown. Add mixture ② then cabbage. Stir to mix well.

1 油1大匙燒熱，入包心菜及鹽1/8小匙，如太乾加水1大匙，略炒軟撈出，擦乾鍋面。

2 油2大匙燒熱，炒香蒜苗，隨入 ① 料炒至肉熟，豆乾微黃，續入調勻的 ② 料炒勻，再加炒好的包心菜翻炒均勻即成。

⅓ lb. (150g) pressed bean curd, sliced

⅓ lb. (150g) Chinese leeks, cut in sections

1. 1 T. soy sauce
   ½ T. sesame oil
   2 T. stock or water

🦐 🦐 🦐

⅓ lb. (150g) bean curd strips

1. 2 t. baking soda
   4 c. water

⅓ lb. (150g) yellow Chinese chives

½ T. minced garlic clove

2. ⅓ t. each: salt, sugar
   ½ T. sesame oil
   2 T. water

豆乾 ·················4兩(150公克)

韭 菜(切段) ·········4兩(150公克)

醬油 ························1大匙
麻油 ·······················1/2大匙
高湯或水 ··················2大匙

🍵 🍵 🍵

干絲 ·················4兩(150公克)

小蘇打 ······················2小匙
水 ····························4杯

韭 黃·················4兩(150公克)

蒜末 ·························1/2大匙

鹽、糖 ···················各1/3小匙
麻油 ·······················1/2大匙
水 ··························2大匙

Pressed Bean Curd & Chinese Leeks

豆乾炒韭菜 (芹菜)

1 Heat 2 T. oil. Stir-fry bean curd until both sides turn golden brown. Add leeks (if celery is used, cut in sections then shred) and stir-fry 20 seconds. Add mixture ❶ ; stir to mix well. Serve.

1 油2大匙燒熱，將豆乾煎炒至兩面呈金黃色後，隨入韭菜 (若使用芹菜，略切段) 炒約20秒，再加調勻的 ❶ 料炒拌均勻即成。

🍵 🍵 🍵

Bean Curd Strips & Chinese Chives

干絲炒韭黃

1 Soak bean curd strips in ❶ until soft (see procedure 1 of p.21). Cut Chinese chives in sections.

2 Heat 2 T. oil. Stir-fry garlic until fragrant; add bean curd strips, then the chives; stir-fry briefly. Add mixture ❷ ; stir to mix well. Serve.

1 干絲放入 ❶ 料內泡軟 (見21頁作法 1)；韭黃切段備用。

2 油2大匙燒熱，炒香蒜，依序入干絲、韭黃略炒，再加 ❷ 料炒拌均勻即成。

¼ lb. (115g) bean curd sheets

1 | 1 t. baking soda
2 c. water

½ lb. (225g) broccoli, cut in pieces

1 T. minced garlic cloves

2 | ⅓ t. salt
1 t. sugar
pepper as desired
½ T. sesame oil
½ c. stock or water

百頁	…………………	3兩(115公克)

1
小蘇打	……………………	1小匙
水	……………………	2杯

靑花菜(切小朶)	…	6兩(225公克)
蒜末	………………………	1大匙

2
鹽	………………………	1/3小匙
糖	………………………	1小匙
胡椒	……………………	少許
麻油	……………………	1/2大匙
高湯或水	…………………	1/2杯

Bean Curd Sheets & Broccoli

玉蘭百頁

1 Bring ❶ to boil then turn off heat immediately. Add bean curd sheets; stir until soft and color changes to white (Soaking time varies from 1 to 20 minutes depending on the brand). Remove and rinse until odor is gone, then cut in strips.

2 Heat 2 T. oil. Stir-fry garlic until fragrant. Add the strips and broccoli then stir-fry briefly. Add mixture ❷. Bring to boil; stir and continue to cook 2 more minutes; remove. Serve.

1 將 ❶ 料燒開即熄火，放入百頁，時時翻拌至呈白色且軟硬適度 (視廠牌不同，泡的時間約由1分鐘到20分鐘不等)，撈出沖洗至無蘇打味後切條。

2 油2大匙燒熱，炒香蒜末，隨入百頁及靑花菜略炒，再加調勻的 ❷ 料燒開，炒拌續煮2分鐘即成。

½ lb. (225g) tofu, cut in pieces

oil for deep-frying

1 total of 1 c. (diced): green & red bell peppers, onion
1 c. diced pineapple

2 ¾ t. salt
½ c. sugar
1 T. cornstarch
⅓ c. each: vinegar, ketchup
½ c. water

½ lb. (225g) tofu, deep-fried (see procedure 1 of above recipe)

1 3 dried chilies, diced
1 t. diced garlic

4 mushrooms, cut in half

2 ½ t. each: salt, sugar, vinegar
1 t. each: cornstarch, sesame oil
2 T. soy sauce
6 T. water

36

豆腐 ·················6兩 (225公克)

炸油 ·····················適量

1 靑、紅椒、洋蔥切丁 ······共1杯
鳳梨丁 ·····················1杯

2 鹽 ·······················³/₄小匙
糖 ·························¹/₂杯
太白粉 ·····················1大匙
醋、番茄醬 ················各¹/₃杯
水 ·························¹/₂杯

炸豆腐 (見上面做法*1*) ········6兩
(225公克)

1 乾辣椒 (切丁) ··············3支
蒜末 ·······················1小匙

洋菇 (切半) ················4個

2 鹽、糖、醋 ···············各¹/₂小匙
太白粉、麻油 ············各1小匙
醬油 ·······················2大匙
水 ·························6大匙

Sweet & Sour Tofu

甜酸豆腐

1 Heat oil for deep-frying. Fry tofu over high heat for 4 minutes until golden brown; remove.

2 Heat 2 T. oil and stir-fry **1** briefly. Add mixture **2** and stir until sauce thickens. Add tofu and serve.

1 炸油燒熱，將豆腐大火炸約4分鐘至金黃色撈出。

2 油2大匙燒熱，將 **1** 料略炒，隨入調勻的 **2** 料炒拌至濃稠狀，再加炸豆腐即成。

Spicy Kung Pao Tofu

宮保豆腐

1 Heat 2 T. oil. Stir-fry **1** until fragrant. Add in mushrooms and stir briefly. Add mixture **2** and stir until sauce thickens. Add tofu and stir to mix well.

1 油2大匙燒熱，炒香 **1** 料，將洋菇略炒，隨入調勻的 **2** 料炒拌至濃稠狀，再加炸好的豆腐拌勻即成。

½ lb. (225g) tofu

1

2 T. dried shrimp, rinsed and minced
4 T. pickled mustard greens (rinsed and minced)
1 T. minced green onion
1 t. minced ginger root

¼ lb. (115g) ground pork, beef, or chicken

2

¼ t. sugar
pepper, sesame oil as desired
½ T. cornstarch
1 T. cooking wine
½ c. stock or water

1 egg white, beaten until foamy.

38

豆腐 ·················6兩 (225公克)	

蝦米 (略洗,剁碎) ········2大匙
榨菜 (略洗,剁碎) ········4大匙
蔥 (切碎) ·················1大匙
薑 (切碎) ·················1小匙

絞肉 (鷄、牛或豬肉) ········3兩
(115公克)

糖 ·····················¼小匙
胡椒、麻油 ·················各少許
太白粉 ···················½大匙
酒 ·······················1大匙
高湯或水 ·················½杯

蛋白 (打發成白雪狀) ········1個

Tofu & Egg White

白雪豆腐

1   Heat 2 T. oil. Stir-fry **1** until fragrant. Add ground pork; stir until cooked and separated. Add tofu and mash tofu with spatula then stir with mixture **2** until it thickens. Finally, stir in egg white then add salt as desired (both dried shrimp and pickled mustard greens contain salt; taste test for saltiness).

1   油2大匙燒熱,炒香 **1** 料,隨入絞肉炒開至熟,續入豆腐並用鍋鏟壓碎,再加調勻的 **2** 料炒拌成濃稠狀,最後放入打好的蛋白拌勻,先試鹹淡再酌量加鹽即成 (因蝦米與榨菜有鹹味)。

½ lb. (225g) tofu

¼ lb. (115g) ground beef, pork, or chicken

1
2 T. minced green onion
½ T. minced garlic clove
½ t. minced ginger root
1 T. hot bean paste or chili paste

2
¼ t. sugar
1 T. cooking wine
1 ½ T. soy sauce
2 t. cornstarch
¾ c. stock or water

3
2 T. chopped fresh garlic or green onion
dash of Szechuan peppercorn powder (optional)

豆腐 ················6兩 (225公克)	
絞肉 (雞、牛或豬肉) ········3兩 (115公克)	

1
蔥 (切碎) ···················2大匙
蒜 (切碎) ··················1/2大匙
薑 (切碎) ··················1/2小匙
辣豆瓣醬或辣椒醬 ········1大匙

2
糖 ······················1/4小匙
酒 ·······················1大匙
醬油 ···················1 1/2大匙
太白粉 ····················2小匙
高湯或水 ··················3/4杯

3
蒜苗或蔥花 ···············2大匙
花椒粉 (無亦可) ···········少許

Ma Pao Tofu

麻婆豆腐

1 Cut tofu in small pieces.

2 Heat 2 T. oil. Stir-fry **1** until fragrant. Add ground pork; stir until the meat is cooked and separated. Add mixture **2** and tofu. Bring to boil and stir until sauce thickens (about 3 minutes). Sprinkle with **3**. Serve.

1 豆腐切小塊。

2 油2大匙燒熱,炒香 **1** 料,入絞肉炒開至熟,再加調勻的 **2** 料及豆腐燒開,炒拌煮至濃稠狀 (約3分鐘),撒入 **3** 料即成。

Sou Tse Tofu

紹子豆腐

1 Exclude hot bean paste from ingredients **1** and increase soy sauce in **2** to 2 1/2 T.. Other ingredients and procedures are the same as "Ma Pao Tofu" above.

1 將 **1** 料內的辣豆瓣醬去除, **2** 料內的醬油改為2 1/2大匙,其他材料及做法如上。

½ lb. (225g) tofu

4 sections green onion, 1" (3cm) long

1 | 1 c. lima beans
½ c. sliced mushrooms

2 | ⅓ t. each: salt, sugar
pepper, sesame oil as desired
2 t. cornstarch
1 T. cooking wine
1 c. stock

½ lb. (225g) soft tofu
½ c. bean curd pouch, diced

1 | ½ c. crab meat (fresh or in can)
8 Chinese pea pods

2 | the same as 2 of above recipe

豆腐(切塊) ·········6兩(225公克)

蔥(3公分長) ·····················4段

蠶豆 ······························1杯
洋菇(切片) ·····················1/2杯

鹽、糖 ······················各1/3小匙
胡椒、麻油 ·················各少許
太白粉 ·····························2小匙
酒 ································1大匙
高湯 ·······························1杯

嫩豆腐(切丁) ······6兩(225公克)

新鮮腐皮(切丁) ···············1/2杯

蟹肉(新鮮或罐頭) ···········1/2杯
豌豆莢 ····························8片

2 料同上

Tofu & Lima Beans

蠶豆燴豆腐

1 Heat 2 T. oil. Stir-fry green onions until fragrant. Add **1** and stir-fry briefly. Add mixture **2** and tofu. Bring to boil and stir 3 minutes until sauce thickens.

1 油2大匙燒熱,炒香蔥,隨入 **1** 料略炒,再加調勻的 **2** 料及豆腐燒開,炒拌煮濃稠狀(約3分鐘)即成。

Tofu & Crab Meat

蟹肉腐皮豆腐

1 Bring bean curd, bean curd pouch and **2** to boil; stir until sauce thickens. Add **1** and bring to another boil. Continue to cook 2 minutes. Serve.

1 將豆腐、新鮮腐皮加 **2** 料燒開,炒拌煮至濃稠狀,隨入 **1** 料再燒開,續煮2分鐘即成。

⅔ lb. (300g) nappa cabbage

½ lb. (225g) Tofu

2 dried scallops

1
½ t. salt
dash of pepper
¾ c. stock or water (with retained
    scallop juice from procedure

2
1 ½ T. cornstarch
2 T. water

大白菜	8兩 (300公克)
豆腐	6兩 (225公克)
乾干貝	2個
鹽	¹/₂小匙
胡椒	少許
高湯或水 (連干貝餘汁)	³/₄杯
太白粉	1 ¹/₂大匙
水	2大匙

Tofu, Scallops & Nappa

干貝白菜豆腐

1 Rinse nappa cabbage; cut both nappa cabbage and tofu in pieces. Soak the scallops in hot water for more than 1 hour or steam 30 minutes until soft. Hand shred scallops. Retain the juice for ingredients **1**.

2 Heat 3 T. oil. Add cabbage stems first, then leaves and stir-fry briefly. Add tofu, scallops and **1**; bring to boil. Stir and continue to cook 3 minutes; add mixture **2**, stir to thicken. Serve.

1 大白菜洗淨切塊，豆腐切塊，乾干貝在熱水內泡軟 (1小時以上) 或蒸軟 (約30分鐘)，用手撕成絲，汁留用。

2 油3大匙燒熱，先放入白菜梗部，再入葉部略炒，再加上豆腐、干貝及 **1** 料燒開，輕炒拌續煮3分鐘，以調勻的 **2** 料勾芡即成。

½ lb. (225g) soft tofu

⅓ lb. (150g) shelled shrimp

1 ⅙ t. salt
1 t. each: cooking wine, cornstarch

1 gherkin cucumber

2 ⅓ t. each: salt, sugar
pepper, sesame oil as desired
2 t. cornstarch
1 c. stock or water

Tofu & Shrimp

蝦仁豆腐

嫩豆腐 ……………6兩 (225公克)

蝦仁 ……………4兩 (150公克)

鹽 …………………………¹/₆小匙
酒、太白粉 ……………各1小匙

小黃瓜 …………………………1條

鹽、糖 …………………各¹/₃小匙
胡椒、麻油 ………………各少許
太白粉 …………………………2小匙
高湯或水 …………………………1杯

1   Cut tofu in pieces. Mix shrimp with **1** ; pare cucumber skin and cut in strips.

2   Heat 2 T. oil. Stir-fry shrimp until cooked; remove.

3   Bring tofu, cucumber and mixture **2** to boil; stir until sauce thickens (about 3 minutes). Add shrimp and stir to mix well; serve.

1   豆腐切塊。蝦仁調入 **1** 料拌勻。小黃瓜去皮切條。

2   油2大匙燒熱，將蝦仁炒熟撈出。

3   將豆腐、黃瓜及 **2** 料燒開，炒拌煮至濃稠狀 (約3分鐘) 後，加入炒熟的蝦仁拌勻即成。

½ lb. (225g) tofu

6 slices ham

6 shelled shrimp

6 fresh scallops

1 salt, cooking wine as desired
1 t. cornstarch

1 T. chopped green onion

2 ⅓ t. salt
pepper, sesame oil as desired
2 t. cornstarch
1 T. cooking wine
1 c. stock or water

豆腐 ················6兩(225公克)	
火腿 ····················6片	
蝦仁 ····················6條	
鮮干貝 ··················6個	
鹽、酒 ················各少許	
太白粉 ················1小匙	
蔥花 ····················1大匙	
鹽 ····················1/3小匙	
胡椒、麻油 ············各少許	
太白粉 ··················2小匙	
酒 ······················1大匙	
高湯或水 ················1杯	

Tofu With Seafood

海鮮豆腐

1 Cut tofu into pieces. Mix shrimp and scallops with mixture **①**.

2 Heat 2 T. oil. Stir-fry green onion until fragrant. Add mixture **②** and tofu, bring to boil. Add ham, shrimp and scallops and bring to another boil. Stir until sauce thickens (about 3 minutes).

1 豆腐切塊。蝦仁、干貝調入 **①** 料拌勻。

2 油2大匙燒熱，炒香蔥，隨入調勻的 **②** 料及豆腐燒開，再入火腿、蝦仁及干貝燒開，炒拌煮至濃稠狀(約3分鐘)即成。

2 tofu, 1/2 lb. (225g)

1/4 lb. (115g) shelled shrimp

1 1/8 t. salt
dash of pepper and sesame oil
1 t. each: cooking wine, cornstarch

2 1/3 t. each: salt, sugar
dash of pepper and sesame oil
1 T. cooking wine
1 1/2 c. stock or water

3 1/2 T. cornstarch
1 T. water

1 T. chopped green onion

bok choy as desired

豆腐2塊	…………	6兩（225公克）
蝦仁	…………	3兩（115公克）

1
鹽	…………	¹/₈小匙
胡椒、麻油	…………	各少許
酒、太白粉	…………	各1小匙

2
鹽、糖	…………	各¹/₃小匙
胡椒、麻油	…………	各少許
酒	…………	1大匙
高湯或水	…………	1¹/₂杯

3
太白粉	…………	¹/₂大匙
水	…………	1大匙

蔥花	…………	1大匙
青江菜	…………	適量

Stuffed Tofu in Wine

溜鑲豆腐

1 Mince shrimp then coat with mixture ❶ to make filling. Blanch bok choy in boiling water until cooked; remove.

2 Diagonally cut each tofu in half then crosswise to make 4 triangles. Scoop out the triangle on one of the cut sides to form a pocket; sprinkle with cornstarch and put in one portion of filling. Follow the same procedures to fill the other 7 triangles.

3 Bring ❷ to boil then add in stuffed tofu; bring to another boil and cook 5 minutes. Lightly thicken with mixture ❸. Sprinkle with green onion and place on a serving plate. Place bok choy around the tofu as garnish.

1 蝦仁剁碎，調入 ❶ 料拌勻成餡。青江菜燙熟備用。

2 每塊豆腐交叉切三角形可切4塊。共8塊在斜面上將豆腐挖出，內撒少許太白粉再將餡塞入抹平，剩餘豆腐同法鑲好備用。

3 將 ❷ 料燒開，放入鑲好的豆腐再燒開，續煮5分鐘，以調勻的 ❸ 料勾成薄汁，撒上蔥花置盤，用燙熟的青江菜圍邊即成。

① Total of 1 lb. (450g): Deep-fried tofu, tofu and pressed bean curd

② 1 T. sugar
¼ c. cooking wine
⅓ c. soy sauce
2 c. stock or water
dash of five-spice powder (optional)

🍃　🍃　🍃

1 lb. (450g) tofu

① 1 t. each: sesame oil, Szechuan peppercorns

② 1 T. fermented black beans
1 T. hot bean paste
1 t. minced ginger

③ 1 c. stock or water
1 t. soy sauce
¼ t. salt

④ 2 t. cornstarch
1 T. water

1	炸豆腐、豆腐、豆乾 ⋯⋯共12兩 (450公克)
2	糖 ⋯⋯⋯⋯⋯⋯⋯⋯⋯⋯⋯1大匙 酒 ⋯⋯⋯⋯⋯⋯⋯⋯⋯⋯⋯¹/₄杯 醬油 ⋯⋯⋯⋯⋯⋯⋯⋯⋯⋯¹/₃杯 高湯或水 ⋯⋯⋯⋯⋯⋯⋯⋯2杯 五香粉(無亦可) ⋯⋯⋯⋯⋯少許

	豆腐 ⋯⋯⋯⋯⋯12兩(450公克)
1	麻油、花椒粒 ⋯⋯⋯⋯各1小匙
2	豆豉、辣豆瓣醬 ⋯⋯⋯各1大匙 薑(切碎) ⋯⋯⋯⋯⋯⋯⋯1小匙
3	高湯或水 ⋯⋯⋯⋯⋯⋯⋯⋯1杯 醬油 ⋯⋯1小匙，鹽⋯⋯¹/₄小匙
4	太白粉 ⋯⋯⋯⋯⋯⋯⋯⋯2小匙 水 ⋯⋯⋯⋯⋯⋯⋯⋯⋯⋯1大匙

Stewed Tofu

滷豆腐

1 Bring **2** to boil; add **1** and bring to another boil. Reduce heat to medium and cook 10 minutes. Remove **1** then sprinkle on the sauce from cooking, sesame oil and chili sauce as desired.

1 將 **2** 料燒開，入 **1** 料再燒開，改中火續煮10分鐘後，取出 **1** 料，隨意淋上煮汁、麻油及辣椒醬食用。

Chili Tofu

辣味豆腐鍋

1 Heat 2 T. oil. Stir-fry **1** in medium heat until fragrant. Remove Szechuan peppercorns. Use remaining oil to stir-fry **2**. Add tofu and **3** then bring to boil; reduce heat to medium and cook 5 minutes. Add mixture **4** to thicken.

1 油2大匙燒熱，中火將 **1** 料炒香，把花椒粒撈出不要，餘油炒香 **2** 料，隨入豆腐及 **3** 料燒開，中火燒煮5分鐘，再加調勻的 **4** 料勾成薄汁即成。

½ lb. (225g) tofu

oil for deep-frying

1. 4 sections green onions, 2.5" (6 cm.) long
2 slices ginger
4 Chinese black mushrooms, pre-softened in cold water (cut in half)

2. 8 slices of bamboo shoots
2 bok choys, cut in half

3. sugar, pepper, sesame oil as desired
2 t. cornstarch
2 T. soy sauce
1 ¼ c. stock or water

豆腐 ·················6兩 (225公克)

炸油 ·······················適量

蔥 (6公分長) ·················4段
薑 ·························2片
香菇 (泡軟、切半) ···········4朵

筍 ·························8片
青江菜 (切半) ···············2棵

糖、胡椒、麻油 ···········各少許
太白粉 ···················2小匙
醬油 ·····················2大匙
高湯或水 ·················1 1/4杯

Tofu in Soy Sauce

紅燒豆腐

1 Pat tofu dry and cut in pieces.

2 Heat oil for deep-frying then fry tofu over high heat 4 minutes until both sides turn golden brown; remove.

3 Heat 1 T. oil and stir-fry ❶ until fragrant. Add ❷ and stir-fry briefly. Add ❸ and tofu; bring to boil. Stir until sauce thickens (about 3 minutes).

1 豆腐拭乾水份,切塊。

2 炸油燒熱,將豆腐大火炸約4分鐘至兩面呈金黃色撈出。

3 油1大匙燒熱,炒香 ❶ 料,隨入 ❷ 料略炒,再加 ❸ 料及炸好的豆腐燒開,炒拌煮至濃稠狀 (約3分鐘) 即成。

½ lb. (225g) Tofu (2 pieces pkg)

oil for deep-frying

1
4 sections green onion, 1" (2cm) long
4 slices ginger root
1 ½ t. chili paste

2
6 slices meat (chicken, beef, or pork)
2 Chinese Black mushrooms, pre-softened in cold water (slices)
6 slices of bamboo shoots

3
1 t. each: sugar, sesame oil
2 t. cornstarch
1 ¼ t. each: soy sauce, oyster sauce (or 2 ½ t. soy sauce)
1 ¼ c. stock or water

豆腐2塊 ··········6兩(225公克)

炸油 ·····························適量

蔥(2公分長) ·····················4段
薑 ·······························4片
辣椒醬 ····················1 ¹/₂小匙

肉(鷄、牛或豬肉) ···········6片
香菇(泡軟,切片) ············2朵
筍 ·······························6片

糖、麻油 ·················各1小匙
太白粉 ·························2小匙
醬油、蠔油 ··········各1 ¹/₄小匙
(或醬油2 ¹/₂小匙)
高湯或水 ·····················1 ¹/₄杯

Home-Style Tofu

家常豆腐

1. Pat tofu dry and horizontally cut each piece of tofu into 3 slices. Diagonally cut the slices in half then crosswise to make 4 triangles. One tofu makes 12 triangular pieces.

2. Heat oil for deep-frying, then fry tofu over high heat 4 minutes until both sides turn golden brown; remove.

3. Heat 2 T. oil then stir-fry ❶ until fragrant. Add ❷ and stir-fry briefly. Add deep fried tofu and mixture ❸ ; bring to boil. Stir 3 minutes until sauce thickens. Serve.

1. 豆腐拭乾水份,每塊橫切3片,再交叉切三角形,一塊可切12片。

2. 炸油燒熱,將豆腐大火炸約4分鐘至兩面呈金黃色撈出。

3. 油2大匙燒熱,炒 ❶ 料,隨入 ❷ 料略炒,再加 ❸ 料及炸好的豆腐燒開,炒拌煮至濃稠狀(約3分鐘)即成。

½ lb. (225g) tofu

oil for deep-frying

1. ¼ c. each, (shredded): onion, celery, carrot, pre-softened Chinese black mushrooms and bamboo shoots

2. 1 t. each: sugar, sesame oil
   2 t. cornstarch
   1 ¼ T. oyster or soy sauce
   1 ¼ c. stock or water

豆腐 ·················6兩（225公克）

炸油 ···························適量

洋蔥、西芹、紅蘿蔔、
香菇、筍 ·············切絲各¼杯

糖、麻油 ···············各1小匙
太白粉 ·····················2小匙
蠔油或醬油 ··········1¼大匙
高湯或水 ···············1¼杯

Golden Rainbow Tofu

五彩豆腐

1 Pat tofu dry and cut in strips.

2 Heat oil then deep-fry tofu over high heat 4 minutes until both sides turn golden brown; remove.

3 Heat 2 T. oil then stir-fry ❶ briefly. Add mixture ❷ and deep-fried tofu; bring to boil. Stir until sauce thickens (about 3 minutes).

1 豆腐拭乾水份，切長條。

2 炸油燒熱，大火將豆腐炸約4分鐘至兩面呈金黃色撈出。

3 油2大匙燒熱，入 ❶ 料略炒，隨入調勻的 ❷ 料及炸好的豆腐燒開，炒拌煮至濃稠狀（約3分鐘）即成。

½ lb. (225g) tofu

oil for deep-frying

1. ¼ lb. (115g) ground chicken, beef or pork
2 T. minced green onion
½ T. minced garlic clove
½ t. minced ginger root
1 t. hot bean or chili paste

2. ½ T. each: sugar, worcester-shire or black vinegar
2 t. cornstarch
1 t. sesame oil
1 ½ T. soy sauce
1 ¼ c. stock or water

3. total of 2 T.: chopped green onions, coriander

豆腐 ················6兩 (225公克)	
炸油 ··························適量	
絞肉 (鷄、牛或豬肉) ········3兩 (115公克)	
蔥 (切碎) ··················2大匙	
蒜 (切碎) ·················$\frac{1}{2}$大匙	
薑 (切碎) ·················$\frac{1}{2}$小匙	
辣豆瓣醬或辣椒醬 ········1小匙	
糖、辣醬油或黑醋 ······各$\frac{1}{2}$大匙	
太白粉 ···················2小匙	
麻油 ·····················1小匙	
醬油 ···················1$\frac{1}{2}$大匙	
高湯或水 ················1$\frac{1}{4}$杯	
蔥花、香菜 ···············共2大匙	

Tofu in Vinegar Sauce

香醋燒豆腐

1   Pat tofu dry and cut in pieces.

2   Heat oil then deep-fry tofu over high heat 4 minutes until both sides turn golden brown; remove.

3   Heat 2 T. oil then stir-fry **1** until fragrant and ground meat is separated and cooked. Add mixture **2** and tofu; bring to boil. Stir until sauce thickens; sprinkle with **3** . Serve.

1   豆腐拭乾水份,切塊。

2   炸油燒熱,將豆腐大火炸約4分鐘至兩面呈金黃色撈出。

3   油2大匙燒熱,炒香 **1** 料至絞肉炒開,再加調勻的 **2** 料及炸好的豆腐燒開,炒拌煮至濃稠狀,撒上 **3** 料即成。

½ lb. (225g) tofu, 2 pieces

oil for deep-frying

¼ lb. (115g) ground chicken, beef, or pork

1 ⎰ ⅛ t. salt
  ⎰ dash of pepper and sesame oil
  ⎰ 1 t. each: cornstarch, cooking wine
  ⎰ 1 T. water

4 sections green onion, 1" (3cm) long

2 ⎰ 1 t. sugar
  ⎰ 1 ½ T. soy sauce
  ⎰ 1 ¼ c. stock or water

3 ⎰ ½ T. cornstarch
  ⎰ 1 ½ T. water

1 T. chopped green onion

Stuffed Tofu

箱子豆腐

豆腐2塊 ……………6兩(225公克)	
炸油 …………………………適量	
絞肉(鷄、牛或豬肉) ………3兩	
(115公克)	

鹽 ……………………………¹/₈小匙	
胡椒、麻油 ………………各少許	
太白粉、酒 …………各1小匙	
水 ……………………………1大匙	

蔥(切3公分長) ………………4段

糖 ……………………………1小匙	
醬油 …………………………1¹/₂大匙	
高湯或水 …………………1¹/₄杯	

太白粉 ………………………¹/₂大匙	
水 ……………………………1¹/₂大匙	

蔥花 …………………………1大匙

1 Mix ground meat thoroughly with ❶ to make filling. Pat tofu dry.

2 Heat oil then deep-fry tofu over high heat 4 minutes until both sides are golden brown. Remove. Horizontally, slice the tofu cube 1/4th thickness from the top; do not cut through, leaving 1/4" intact. Scoop out the tofu to form a pocket and stuff with filling.

3 Heat 1 T. oil. Stir-fry green onion sections until fragrant. Add ❷ and tofu; bring to boil. Cover and cook over low heat 10 minutes until liquid is reduced by half. Add mixture ❸ to thicken; stir. Sprinkle with chopped green onion; serve.

1 絞肉調入 ❶ 料拌勻成餡；豆腐拭乾水份備炸。

2 炸油燒熱,將豆腐大火炸約4分鐘至金黃色撈出。將豆腐在厚度¹/₄處片開,約留0.5公分不切斷,掀開在內面挖成凹狀,鑲入肉餡備用。

3 油1大匙燒熱,炒香蔥段,隨入 ❷ 料及豆腐燒開,改小火蓋鍋,續煮10分鐘至湯汁剩約一半,再加調勻的 ❸ 料勾芡,撒上蔥花即成。

½ lb. (225g) tofu

4 T. cornstarch or flour

oil for deep-frying

1 1 t. each: sugar, vinegar
2 T. soy sauce
1 t. minced garlic clove
1 minced chili (optional)

2 1 t. salt
⅛ t. pepper

1 2 T. soy sauce
½ c. stock or water
2 T. chopped green onion
4 T. daikon paste or dried shaved
bonito

豆腐 ·················6兩 (225公克)

太白粉或麵粉 ··············4大匙

炸油 ··························適量

1
糖、醋 ·················各1小匙
醬油 ·····················2大匙
蒜末 ·····················1小匙
辣椒 (切碎，無亦可) ········1條

2
鹽 ·······················1小匙
胡椒 ···················$1/_8$小匙

1
醬油 ·····················2大匙
高湯或水 ················$1/_2$杯
蔥花 ·····················2大匙
白蘿蔔泥或柴魚片 ········4大匙

Deep-fried Tofu

炸豆腐

1   Pat tofu dry; cut into 12 pieces then evenly coat with cornstarch.

2   Heat oil, add tofu and deep-fry over high heat 4 minutes until both sides are golden brown. Remove. Serve with either **1** or **2** as dipping sauce.

1   將豆腐拭乾水份，切成12塊，沾裹太白粉。

2   炸油燒熱，入豆腐用大火炸約4分鐘至呈金黃色即撈出，任選 **1** 、 **2** 沾料沾食。

Tofu in Daikon Sauce

泡湯豆腐

1   Place deep-fried tofu from above recipe into mixture **1** ; Serve.

1   依上面作法 *1* 、 *2* 將豆腐炸好，放入調勻 **1** 料內即成。

1. total of ¼ lb. (115g) ground chicken, beef, or pork, shelled shrimp (minced)

2. ⅛ t. salt
pinch of pepper and sesame oil as desired
1 t. each: cooking wine, corn-starch
1 T. water

2 tofu, ½ lb. (225g)

3. 1 egg
½ c. flour
4 T. water

oil for deep-frying

絞肉（鷄、牛或豬肉）、
蝦仁（剁碎）……共3兩(115公克)

鹽 ……………………¹/₈小匙
胡椒、麻油 ……………各少許
酒、太白粉 ……………各1小匙
水 ……………………1大匙

豆腐2塊………………………6兩

蛋 ……………………………1個
麵粉 …………………………¹/₂杯
水 ……………………………4大匙

炸油 …………………………適量

Deep-fried Layered Tofu

千層豆腐

1   Mix ❶ and ❷ well to make filling. Mix ❸ to make a flour paste.

2   Cut each tofu into 3 slices. Sprinkle cornstarch on first slice then spread the filling on it. Place second slice of tofu on top. Continue to assemble layers until each stack has 3 layers of tofu and 2 layers of filling. Coat each stack evenly with flour paste.

3   Heat oil, then deep-fry tofu over medium heat 7 minutes until both sides are golden brown. Remove. Cut the tofu in pieces. Serve with any desired dipping sauce, i.e. soy sauce, oyster sauce or ketchup, etc.

1   ❶料加 ❷料攪拌均勻成餡，❸料調勻成蛋糊。

2   每塊豆腐切3薄片；豆腐一片撒上少許太白粉，塗一層餡加一片豆腐，再撒太白粉及塗餡，如此反覆做成豆腐3層，餡2層，共做2個；炸前均勻塗上蛋糊。

3   炸油燒熱，入豆腐用中火炸約7分鐘至金黃色肉熟即撈出，切塊置盤，沾醬油、蠔油或番茄醬食用。

⅓ lb. (150g) tofu

¼ lb. (115g) ground chicken, beef or pork

1.
⅓ t. salt
½ t. sugar
½ egg white
1 t. each (minced): green onion, ginger root
1 T. cornstarch
½ t. sesame oil

½ c. bread crumbs

oil for deep-frying

68

豆腐 ················4兩(150公克)	
絞肉(鷄、牛或豬肉) ········3兩	
	(115公克)
鹽 ··················¹/₃小匙	
糖 ··················¹/₂小匙	
蛋白 ·················¹/₂個	
蔥、薑末 ··············各1小匙	
太白粉 ················1大匙	
麻油 ·················¹/₂小匙	
麵包粉 ················¹/₂杯	
炸油 ··················適量	

Tofu Balls

豆腐丸子

1   Mash tofu then mix with ground meat and ❶. Form 16 balls. Coat the balls with bread crumbs.

2   Heat oil then deep-fry balls over medium heat 3 minutes until golden brown and cooked. Remove, then serve with ketchup and pepper salt.

1   豆腐壓成泥狀，加絞肉及 ❶ 料拌勻，揉成16個丸子，沾裹麵包粉。

2   炸油燒熱，入丸子用中火炸約3分鐘至金黃色肉熟即撈出，可沾番茄醬或椒鹽食用。

1. ¼ lb. (115g) fish paste or shrimp paste
   ¼ lb. (115g) ground pork

2. ¼ c. mashed tofu
   ½ c. minced onion
   ¼ c. minced carrot

3. ⅙ t. salt
   1 ½ t. sugar
   dash of pepper and sesame oil
   ½ T. each: cooking wine, corn-starch

   3 sheets of dried bean curd skin, 6"x 8"(15cmx20cm)

4. 2 T. flour
   2 T. water

   oil for deep-frying

1	魚漿或蝦漿 ········3兩(115公克)	
	豬絞肉 ··············3兩(115公克)	
2	豆腐(壓碎) ······················¹/₄杯	
	洋蔥(切碎) ······················¹/₂杯	
	紅蘿蔔(切碎) ···················¹/₄杯	
3	鹽 ···························¹/₆小匙	
	糖 ·························1 ¹/₂小匙	
	胡椒、麻油 ··················各少許	
	酒、太白粉 ··············各¹/₂大匙	
	乾腐皮(15公分×20公分) ···3張	
4	麵粉 ·······························2大匙	
	水 ·······························2大匙	
	炸油 ·····························適量	

Bean Curd Rolls

腐皮捲(鷄捲)

1 Mix ①, ② and ③ well and divide into 3 portions (filling). Mix ④ and set aside.

2 Evenly spread a portion of filling on each bean curd skin; then roll to form a baton. Seal with mixture ④ then cut in 2 sections.

3 Heat oil then deep-fry bean curd rolls in medium heat 6 minutes until cooked and crispy. Remove and cut in small sections. Serve.

■ Ready-made fish paste is available in most supermarkets. If dried bean curd skin is too dry, cover it with wet cloth until soft then use.

1 將 ①、② 及 ③ 料全部攪拌均勻成餡,分成3等份。④ 料調勻成麵糊。

2 乾腐皮放入一份餡,捲成長條狀,以麵糊黏住封口,依次捲好,再分切二段。

3 炸油燒熱,入鷄捲用中火炸約6分鐘至皮酥肉熟即撈出,切小段後置盤。

■ 魚漿可買現成的。腐皮如太乾,可覆蓋濕巾待柔軟後再使用。

2 tofu, ½ lb. (225g)

¼ lb. (115g) shelled shrimp

1
⅛ t. salt
dash of pepper and sesame oil
1 t. each: cooking wine, cornstarch

2
2 T. shredded green onion
dash of coriander and chili

1 ½ T. each: oil, soy sauce

豆腐2塊 ⋯⋯⋯⋯6兩 (225公克)

蝦仁 ⋯⋯⋯⋯⋯⋯3兩 (115公克)

| 鹽 ⋯⋯⋯⋯⋯⋯⋯⋯⋯1/8小匙
| 胡椒、麻油 ⋯⋯⋯⋯⋯各少許
| 酒、太白粉 ⋯⋯⋯⋯各1小匙

| 蔥 (切絲) ⋯⋯⋯⋯⋯⋯2大匙
| 香菜或辣椒 ⋯⋯⋯⋯⋯少許

沙拉油、醬油 ⋯⋯⋯各1 1/2大匙

Tofu Stuffed With Shrimp

蒸蝦鑲豆腐

1 Chop shrimp then mix well with ① to make filling.

2 Cut each tofu into 4 pieces; (makes 8 pieces). Scoop out the pieces and sprinkle with cornstarch then stuff with filling.

3 Steam tofu pieces over high heat for 6 minutes; remove. Sprinkle with ②. Pour on hot oil then soy sauce.

1 蝦仁剁碎,調入 ① 料拌勻成餡。

2 豆腐一塊切4塊,共8小塊。挖出豆腐,內撒少許太白粉,再將餡塞入抹平,依次將豆腐鑲好備用。

3 鑲好的豆腐置蒸盤,大火蒸6分鐘後取出,上置 ② 料,淋上燒熱的沙拉油,再澆上醬油即成。

1 ½ lb. (225g) soft tofu, mashed
   total of ⅓ lb. (150g): ground
      meat, shelled shrimp (minced)

2 ½ t. salt
   pinch of pepper
   1 t. each: cooking wine, sesame
      oil
   1 egg white
   ½ T. cornstarch

嫩豆腐 (壓碎) ……6兩 (225公克)
絞肉 (雞、牛或豬肉)、
蝦仁 (剁碎) ……共4兩 (150公克)

鹽 …………………………¹/₂小匙
胡椒 ……………………………少許
酒、麻油 ……………………各1小匙
蛋白 ………………………………1個
太白粉 …………………………¹/₂大匙

Steamed Tofu Cake

蒸豆腐糕

1 Mix ❶ and ❷ well and place in a steam bowl. Bring water to boil and steam over high heat 30 minutes until meat is cooked. Garnish with chopped green onion, coriander, or other garnish as desired.

1 ❶料加 ❷料拌勻置蒸碗，水燒開大火蒸30分鐘至肉熟，可撒些蔥花或香菜，或隨喜好擺盤飾。

4 bean curd sheets ("Bai Ye")

1
1 t. baking soda
2 c. water

2
total of ¼ lb. (115g): shredded shrimp (minced), ground pork
⅛ t. salt
dash of pepper and sesame oil as desired
1 t. each: cooking wine, cornstarch

3
⅛ t. salt
2 T. each (shredded): pre-softened Chinese black mushrooms, cooked bamboo shoots
¾ c. stock or water
1 t. each: cornstarch, sesame oil

百頁	4張
小蘇打	1小匙
水	2杯
蝦仁 (剁碎)、豬絞肉	共3兩 (115公克)
鹽	1/8小匙
胡椒、麻油	各少許
酒、太白粉	各1小匙
鹽	1/8小匙
泡軟的香菇絲、熟筍絲	各2大匙
高湯或水	3/4杯
太白粉、麻油	各1小匙

Stuffed Bean Curd Rolls
蒸百頁捲

1   Soak bean curd sheets in mixture ① to soften (see procedure 1 of p.35).

2   Mix ② well to make filling; divide into 4 portions. Place one portion of filling on one opened bean curd sheet; roll the sheet to form a baton. Repeat 3 more times. Steam the rolls in boiling water, over high heat, for 10 minutes. Remove and cut each roll in half; arrange on a serving plate.

3   Bring ③ to boil. Stir until sauce thickens. Pour liquid over the bean curd rolls; serve.

■   If bean curd sheet is too thin, use two sheets for one roll...

1   將百頁放入 ① 料內泡軟 (見35頁作法 *1*)

2   將 ② 料拌勻成餡,分成4等份。百頁攤開,放入一份餡,捲成長條狀,依次捲好置蒸盤,水開大火蒸10分鐘取出,切半置盤。

3   將 ③ 料燒開炒拌煮至濃稠狀,淋在百頁捲上即成。

■   如百頁很薄,可二張疊在一起使用。

❑ Index

索引

More From Wei-Chuan Publishing 味全叢書

Cookbooks :

(All cookbooks are bilingual English/Chinese unless footnoted otherwise)

Chinese Appetizers & Garnishes
Chinese Cooking, Favorite Home Dishes
Chinese Cooking For Beginners (Revised) [1]
Chinese Cooking Made Easy
Chinese Cuisine
Chinese Cuisine-Szechwan Style
Chinese Cuisine-Taiwanese Style
Chinese Dim Sum
Chinese One Dish Meals
Chinese Seafood [2]
Chinese Snacks (Revised)
Favorite Chinese Dishes
Great Garnishes
Healthful Cooking
Japanese Cuisine
Low Cholesterol Chinese Cuisine
Mexican Cooking Made Easy [3]
Microwave Cooking I, Chinese Style
Microwave Cooking II, Chinese Style
Noodles, Chinese Home-Cooking
Noodles, Classical Chinese Cooking
Rice, Chinese Home-Cooking
Rice, Traditional Chinese Cooking
Thai Cooking Made Easy
Vegetarian Cooking

Small Cookbook Series :

Vegetables [2]
Beef [2]
Chicken [2]
Tofu! Tofu! Tofu!
Very! Very! Vegetarian!
Soup! Soup! Soup!

Carving Tools

Videos [4] :

Chinese Garnishes I
Chinese Garnishes II
Chinese Stir-Frying, Beef
Chinese Stir-Frying, Chicken
Chinese Stir-Frying, Vegetables

[1] Also available in English/Spanish, French/Chinese, and German/Chinese
[2] English and Chinese are separate editions
[3] Also available in English/Spanish
[4] English only

食譜系列
(如無數字標註,即爲中英對照版)

拼盤與盤飾
實用家庭菜
實用中國菜 [1] (修訂版)
速簡中國菜
中國菜
四川菜
台灣菜
飲茶食譜
簡餐專輯
海鮮專輯 [2]
點心專輯
家常100
盤飾精選
健康食譜
日本料理
均衡飲食
墨西哥菜 [3]
微波爐食譜
微波爐食譜 II
麵,家常篇
麵,精華篇
米食,家常篇
米食,傳統篇
泰國菜
素食

味全小食譜:

牛肉 [2]
鷄肉 [2]
蔬菜 [2]
豆腐
家常素食
湯

雕花刀

錄影帶 [4]

盤飾 I
盤飾 II
炒菜入門,牛肉
炒菜入門,鷄肉
炒菜入門,蔬菜

[1] 中英、中法、中德、英
[2] 中文版及英文版
[3] 中英版及英西版
[4] 英文版

Wei-Chuan Cookbooks can be purchased in the U.S.A., Canada and twenty other countries worldwide • Wei-Chuan Publishing • 1455 Monterey Pass Road, # Monterey Park, CA 91754, U.S.A. • Tel: (213)261-3880 • Fax: (213) 261-3299
味全食譜在台、美、加及全球二十餘國皆有發行 • 味全出版社有限公司 • 台北市仁愛路4段28號2樓 • Tel: (02) 702-1148 • Fax: (02) 704-2729